The Winter Sun

Jean Esteve

My thanks to the journals that first published some of these poems:

Basalt, Boston Review, Brooklyn Review, Caveat Lector, Confluence, Confrontation, Eclipse, Exquisite Corpse, Fine Madness, Fireweed, Folio, Fulcrum, Hubbub, Hunger Mountain, Indefinite Space, The Iowa Review, Madison Review, Mudfish, Poetry Bay, Presa, Seattle Review, Tuesday, Wisconsin Review, Zone 3

To my friends Ruth and Ruth

CONTENTS

DIDN'T I SING

Every Love Affair a Snare

       This I was born knowing --
       Every coming has its going,
       Every sweet its stomachache,
       Every boy his false face.

From the radio come reports of heavy storms in the
south.
I can look out the window and tell you as much,
a slow sucking away of afternoon light.
Crows huddle in the fir's lower branch.
Gulls chalk wheels of warning on the darkened sky.

       This I will die having --
       relentless craving,
       rumpled blankets on the bed,
       what he meant by what he said.

Song

Didn't I sing to you, din't I sing
leaves from their trees, and didn't I bring
sparrows down, too, until the country
lost summer, turned sullen. Didn't you hear me?

What did you think makes your roadside so barren
except it be my relentless passion
for song. I was born with north wind in my voice.
I had no choice.

Dear boy, I had no choice.

No Valentine

Like a thief, I wormed my way
        into your office,
crawled inside your file drawers,
        checked out "J" for Jeanie.

I should have guessed the skinny folder
        held only an E mail list
of puns, some funny-papers, a recipe
for boiled potatoes, but no valentine, no porn.

Bless me, Father, I have sinned
        when like a worm I thieved
his potted tree of tangerines,
        so cankered, I, by fury.

My Dress

Look at my dress
my flowered dress
the puff of its sleeves
velvet ribbon at the waist
pearly buttons divide my breasts
look at my dress.
Enjoy the red and yellow
of its embroideries
and how the flowing skirt
whispers in the wind.
See the way lace
at the neck frames my face
no -- look at the dress
only at the dress
look only, only at my dress.

Stranger

I wonder who it might have been
took my hand
in the alley back of Macy's Saturday.
He said he was the peppered moth
come out of hiding since the soot
of industry had chased his friends away.
I don't believe him.

Beach Party

One of us said he saw her
          clinging to a rock.

July. A beach bonfire. Beer and singing.

Questioned further why nobody leapt to help,
          called for help, reported to authority:

Mosquitoes. A vague bellyache. Woodsmoke
                              in our eyes,
stinging.

And she was needy. This seemed nothing new.

Always flinging greedy arms around someone,
                    sticky, pertinacious, yes, we
agreed

the clingiest girl any of us ever knew.

The Small Box

What is this hidden
in the small box?
In the small box
what am I given?

Only a ring
nestled in cotton.
He hasn't forgotten
to buy me a ring.

Then what's on his mind
when he stares at the floor?
When his eyebrows lower
like a boding windstorm?

Oh, what's in the brown sack
clenched in his fist?
A litter of kits
he's drowned and brought back.

What is this hidden?
What's in the wind?
For my coward kisses
a sack of dead kittens.

Drummer

A man came to my door selling -- what could that have been?
have been?
A boxful of plastic shapes, he rang and rang until I let
him in.

Most of them were very red but yellow was in there,
too,
cubed and curled, both short and long, alive and still,
in fact a perfect bouil-

labaisse of temptations. He said that the price was
steep
nor were all the pieces up for sale, and those I bought
I'd have to keep

secret from my husband. "You do have secrets,
ma'am?"
No, I have no secrets, nor husband, nor wherewithal.
In fact I am

not interested in knickknacks no matter how red.
To my delight he fell down on the floor and bawled at
what I said.

The very next day I carved a sign proclaiming:
"Evermore,
All Drummers and Their Likenesses are Welcome
Through This Door."

Last Seen

I'm looking up and down for that joker-of-the-road,
                    has't seen?
Last seen drunk, he was by-productly
                monosyllabic, glassy-eyed, who cares?
One sound at a time's enough for me
cooped up as I am on this barren acre
            of head-and-heart and tomato-soup-can pain.
loop-o, he goes forth anywhere he choose-o's,
                    has't heard word of?
Were it not for that infernal promise of return
            in a halo of happiness,
dragging presents wrapped in tissue, tied with bows,
you'd never find me curled around my toes, so
                        pinioned
by safety-pin ideas, what to buy from the grocery,
what to name the cat,
            I'd be away,
I'd be on the road away. Say what.

Trouble

    Where do you go, Dick Andrew, Dick Andrew
when you leave me?
    your black knit cap pulled down below your
eyebrows,
    when wind and snow have blurred the streetlights
into golden halos,
    and all the doors are barred with iron grates.
    The alleys are hapless, you know that, better yet
than I do,
    and shutters make philosophers of thieves.

        Here on the twenty-eighth floor
        the apartment has been cleared of furniture,
            not a picture left on the wall,
            not a glimmer from the ceiling bulb.

    Dick Andrew: "If the bareness of the rooms gets
overbearing,
            I'll show you where to find twenty-
seven flights of stairs."

    Trouble doesn't bother emptiness,
    but slides up grimy stairwells to where idle stars
collect.
    Where idle stars collect there trouble goes and
stars collide.

A brilliance made me and Dick Andrew in its image once,
    and ever since I've stretched my hands out to its kindnesses,
    always to find trouble in my fist.

Three Boys

Three boys adore me.
We sit in mama's parlor.
Jack looks at his watch.
Dick rises from the couch.
Joey gives a monstrous yawn.
Then they're gone.

Two Boys

Two boys loved me
and I loved two boys back,
reluctantly Dick Andrew
and joyfully and with promises to Jack.

Two boys loved me
dark and light.
Jack kissed me by Alsea Bay
and Dick stole up to my room at night.

Two boys loved me,
drove me wild.
Jack bought me roses
but I had Dick Andrew's child.

Two boys loved me,
then both stopped.
Jack prefers his whisky now
and something happened that Dick Andrew died.

Verse

There were three boys who loved me true
named Richard, Ricky and Dick Andrew.
Richard lied, poor Ricky died,
and foolish Dick, he made me his bride.
So that was the end of my three lovers true,
Richard, Ricky and Dick Andrew.

Spectrum

Red sits at one end of the visible spectrum.
(My end, I will add, parenthetically.)
I paid the gate at the county fair
in early September expecting pumpkins but none
were there.
Flowers, jam, and health care instructions
proliferated; some lady said
I must wait, my dear, for what I most wanted,

and sure enough later they came,
piled high in the Safeway for only a dollar,
for just a buck I might take one home.

That done, I found I was not finished waiting.
Sunshine comes silky and thin in November,
like lady's lingerie.

My underwear flaps overnight on the clothesline,
exhibitionists haughtily spilling my secrets
to deaf stars, those ghosts pale gold.

Nothing exceeds the speed of star's light,
though we try and try, it's always in vain.
Some men behave decently, some never will,
and the hills are kept green by the winter rain.

The Safeway parking lot floods every year
when the storms expect their trees to be there.
Poor rain, almost blind by the grayness of days.
In a national forest I met this woodsman

whose manners were crude, but whose eyes were so
blue
that I let him take me then and there
and I let him marry me, too.

With a big dressy wedding expectancy ends,
        in laundry romance, in dishwater splash!
for we live under ultra-violet light
where no one can see us and only the mailman
calls on us here.
        -- This little verse is sent your way
        to wish you a happy anniversary --.
light so purple it bruises the air
light as slow as a drug.

Claire's Husband

I would marry your husband, Claire,
if two moons rose huge on the horizon,
if for every summer sun there were another sun
        and under that glare
tulips bloomed twice in the garden,
        first red, then yellow.
Claire, I would marry your husband,
        poor, bereft fellow
slumping forlorn at the foot of my stair,
if I had a second heart and gloom to spare.

Whose

Sticking to your feet as our disjunction peaks,
        that faithful pooch called Whose --
whose idea, whose money, whose big pillow, who's
        not funny anymore.

You had an opportunity to choose and chose
        wrong. You lose, my dear.

Bow-wow. He tears the room apart
        and chaos follows,
floor a mess of shredded paper,
            feathers, kapok, soft unto my soles.

From now on I can walk out anywhere.

Out of Water

That man rose slow from the Pacific sea again,
        all skull and bulbous nose blubbering salty
water,
then the chin, round and smooth as an infant's sweet
behind,
        arms, chest, and not a hair on them, either,

then the belly full of the fish of the ocean,
        its round eye closed and unconcerned,
then the legs and that thing between them,
        He sang olu-lu-lu, but I never understood
those words.

Then he heaved up his huge feet and slid along
        easy toward me up the swells and down the
troughs.
Were it not for our baby nestled in my womb
        I should have fled in terror and hid behind the
rocks.

Rhyme

I had a sweet babe and gave it no name.
It snuggled for milk but the tit was dry.
I opened my mouth to try to explain
and down went the sweet baby. Bye-bye.

The Saved Baby

Such a tall man bends over the baby
and bends his intent and intelligent eyes
upon the bared heart of the baby.
His hands are doing what they have been taught;
they sew, with mother-like quilting stitches
two dacron patches
over the holes in the baby's heart.

> this line feeds the baby
> this line breathes the baby
> this line bleeds the baby
> and this leads new blood
> toward its new course.

Meadow

You whiten the meadow as corn lily, tarweed and
stinging phacelia
whitens the hillside, your dress
whitens the meadow in the morning, Genevieve.

As the hillside somersaults down to the river
whose white sand stumbles toward the whitecaps of
the ocean, then for its bed,
your dress rolls over white knees, Genevieve.

In the meadow, on the hillside, Genevieve,
in Sunday clothes picks wildflowers for a wreath.
Her aunts call in vain, "Jenny, dear, it's time to go.
The Lord awaits and we're due any minute now."

April Nearing

April nearing. This measured allowance
of daffodils breaking through cracks in the pavement,
skunk cabbage making the swamped woods buoyant
    and lilac sticks bud-laden.

April nearing. This sense of clairvoyance,
this feeling that we aren't meant to be present
at all, but butt-ins, an accident
    in fact, and a bad one.

How We Live

Modern I live
In a modern home
One wall a window
To frame flocks of crows.

In a modern home
There grow motives
To frame flocks of crows.
a) They darken rooms.

There grow motives
For instance like mushrooms.
a) They darken rooms.
b) I'll remark no further.

For instance like mushrooms
He lives on dirt.
b) I'll remark no further
About how he thrives.

He lives on dirt
And never worries
About how he thrives.
They're all like that

And never worry.
Stars spackle their ceiling.
They're all like that.
I look up to heavy beams.

Stars spackle their ceiling
While my roof hangs low.
I look up to heavy beams
When blackbirds cloud my window.

In a modern home
I look upward to heavy beams.
a) They darken the rooms.
b) I'll remark no further.

AH ME, FREEDOM

Marooned

This is my island, my coconut tree.
Pirates dragged me here. I shrieked
and bellowed for help. You
had other more solemn things to do,
like bringing coffee and muffins on a breakfast tray
up to your mother every day.
I tell you those pirates were mean and glum,
but they said that if I cooked for them
they'd leave me alone, and so I did,
and so they died, one by one.
I buried them under this coconut tree
which now bears huge, well-fertilized fruit
of any flavor that I choose,
at present it's muffins-and-coffee.
You say your mama ran off and wed
some old coot, bald and bowlegged
and now you're longing to visit me.
Do so. Soon.
I raise pet sharks in my lagoon.

St. Him

He wears his halo
comfortably,
it is a perfect fit,
and every word
comes from his mouth
drops hints of how he earned it.

He wears it with
such nonchalance
that sometimes it slips loose,
takes all my strength
of will power not
to tighten up that noose.

The Terrier

I have to hide from the terrier.
Revealer sunlight heartbroken by leaves
collapses in grief to the ground,
transforming the earth to a green-gold-brown river.
I have to hide from the terrier.

I have to hide from the terrier.
In silent compliance to laws of the sea
I wade in and in until drowned
by the wonderful affliction disguising my fur.
I have to hide from the terrier.

Motels

      What I have done with all this money
has evened the edges.   In the desert I stopped
at a large motel with a high peaked roof under a coin
   moon.
      The pool was flat.   Nobody swam in it that
   time of year,
that time of night.   Dolores, the towels were white.
      Last time they were pinkish, remember, and
   frayed,
when you were still in the fray, and our feet hit
cracked linoleum, the sink taps spit, and the toilet
   hummed.
      Oh, Dolores, all fringes and zigzags,
I have trimmed and straightened everything.   I
   walked smoke blue
motel carpet. I heated the room by turning a dial.
      We were chasing down doom, Dolores, you
   found it,
hidden in hedges the glistening frisbee that you
   refused
to return to me.

The Long Bridge

The long bridge loosens.

Tired of its beauty,
sky flakes and falls away
from the spaces in its tracery,
and winds which serenade
through the silver filagree
change key.

At either of its ends
rippled water shilly-shallies
with the restless soil and sighs
like a mother unamused
by the whims of her children
when the long bridge loosens.

Midwinter

Mud-tide, midwinter,
    pocked silver and umber,
the crows and gulls humbled
    below the great heron
who fishes in Tillamook Bay.

Bridge lights glow orange,
    the car headlights yellow,
while windshield wipers go
    swish-swish-swish
on their way across Tillamook Bay.

I crouch by the trestle,
    hunched in my overcoat,
puzzled by cars, herons and gulls,
    wishing that I were anywhere far,
far from Tillamook Bay.

The Wind

Why does the wind
sigh and whimper through the dune grass
these November evenings
when all she has of hindrance
bends before her as before a queen.

"Ah, me, freedom, freedom," she keens.

Away

When I rode on my thumb
away from town
the only cars to come by
were northward bound.

More north, more north, more north sped I.

Now I find
I don't miss your sun.
In place of friends
I have shadow and ice.

More boreal, more boreal I have become.

Ties

The leash knotted, turned short,
inhibiting our daily walk.
I tossed it.

The I.D., the rabies tags
jingled. Jingling's for cats.
I lost those metallic stats.

The collar tightened as he grew,
enough to choke the poor pooch.
I lost the noose.

That cute pup who for a while
stayed by my side, so amiable --
I've gone and lost the little fella.

Hesitations

This wind cuts our skin
and it's ten below.
Ought we to go?

Your children wail and keen.
My dogs bay.
Oughtn't we stay?

The road's ruts are deep
and slick with ice.
Maybe think twice.

No! No! No!
We're off and away.
Greetings, solstice!

Cross Country

Where Nevada is desert
late afternoon through nightfall
color changes by the second
reshaping mesas and the far Sierra.

Herons and pelicans
don't know what to make of such mutations.
Their soaring turns to flutter
and I myself wonder what's the matter.

I've traveled this route twenty times
across the great width of our America,
my mother on one coast,
my dear on the other,

and always I notice this same consternation of birds.
I know, I know, I've heard
that drowsy driving risks your life and car.
I've been okay so far

yet the pleasure of melting with the road.
with static on the radio
and all this now purple, now blue, now red,
is irresistible.

Besides, neither mother nor dear thought of the cost
of a desert motel,
one having never left the snug of New England,
the other, the California scene, as it were.

Turtles are more accustomed
to the kaleidoscopy of their home
and frolic in the open
with salamanders, salamanders

in their element, of course,
having uncles aunts and cousins
full of the same color tricks.
The mountains stay where they are put

tumbling and stretching in place.
I neither leave nor approach them.
We have made a covenant
not to interfere with one another.

As sky lowers,
I look out upon ten thousand prospects,
rivals bent on beguiling
thousand ten thousand of my cells.

So it is that I sit in this car
belted to the seat
and lift my foot off the accelerator
and turn the key.

Mother is not a forgiving sort,
but she can learn,
and lovers are available
surely, at every turn

in any desert town.

The Restless Sister

This spot we're on is hellish far from anywhere
and any other where is there I wish we were.

                    So says the restless sister

as she drifts by me on her island of ice.
Blue-white it is.
She warms her family with a cigarette lighter.

The baby is quiet, the toddlers subdued.
She has at least learned motherhood. Dutifully,
legs steady, feet firm at the tideline,

I toss out my fishline, hook onto the tassel
of her tasseled cap. Dropping the Bic,
she clutches it close.

                    Thus they are guided to shore.

This is farther than we were before.

Sullen now sulks the restless sister.

Sunshine's what she needs. I give her mine
and she's reluctant but instantly transformed,
a fashion model swathed in saffron. She struts

                    while I baby-sit the kids.

I often use my virtue to offend.

The restless sister rises in a fury
bending the horizon with her height,
bending even heaven. So this is the every where
that you had in store,

The sister snarls, baring restless teeth,
and me here neither over nor beneath her.

Only when the children try to bite me
do I lower my long eyelashes
onto the landscape, a long strand
of varicolored grains of sand.
.
The single vertical is a torn abandoned beach
umbrella
                    flapping.

It is here we must inter
the ashes of our father
I tell her, before ever he gets born.

December

Nighttime all day long
        that an arc
        of wind off the bay
        slams rain
against the metal of my brave car

        unafraid
        is it
        of the wet black road
        of the nearby hill
        so shadowed.

For a Christmas song
on the radio
and Christmas lights
with haloes

then a warm café
open late
and a laughing waitress
telling jokes.

Encounter

                if it happens in open prairie
be happy. The quick-changing shadows
like transient friends
are helpful the short while you need them.

Everywhere rhythms,
mute colors mutating, matte gold
to gray green to milky blue-purple,
fuse your surprise to their music.

But in rainforest,
moss looping branches above you
or grabbing your shoe-print like trenchant detectives.

if it's here your heart clutches,
where blackberry thorns are magenta
and skunk cabbage burns in the swamp,

if it's here
you're in luck

for no hooty owl, no carol, no psalm
nothing will soften the stun.

I Will Be Kind

I will be kind to bilious men
for whom the boulevard
is just a tarry smear of gloom.
I'll give them room, and if one's bent
on leading our whole line of cars
away, across, around, ahead,
I'll nod him on as well,

for I've had my own illnesses
and, to tell the truth,
have yet to find a final cure
for aches and gripes and tics,
yet those in front and those behind me,
those on either side,
have not leaned too hard on their horns,
have kept their fingers in their fists
when the road shone black as it unwrapped
its awful gift to all of us.

Henry Smith Bridge

If you use the back road
you'll need to go over
the bridge we call Henry Smith Bridge
whose feet are deep in blackberry briars
and bed and all on the road to decay.

Who Henry Smith was
nobody remembers
but word is that he met his bad end
on the bed and is buried deep in the briars.
It's up to yourself to believe this or not.

Money's been tight
for the last twenty years
and the government's not making bridge repairs.
It's up to yourself how you want to chance it,
Henry Smith or the city traffic.

Return

I come back to you like this—
dressed in my barnacle dress.

Painstaking, I've been, acquiring it.
Note, not a hint

of our beloved gaud and glitter,
no yarny angora to swindle your fingers.

It's settled, then.
We don't have to speak of it again.

You won't ask about my prolongd cruise
or demand to know where I left my clothes,

how wild I was asea—
only smile if you can, and welcome me

inside.
And it subsides—

the hunger for color, the scratchiness,
as one gets used to barnacles.

AS IF STARS WERE FRIENDLY

Not a Pipe

this is not a pipe
          he wrote in french
                    in pretty script
                              indeed
                    beneath
          the picture of a pipe
so nicely done in paint
          whose shape, color, size
denied the title and implied
                              otherwise

oh yes it is a pipe a pipe a pipe
it really is a pipe we piped our brief
across the water to Magritte

Nightwatch

If tonight
would hide its hunger
only for politeness' sake
as it slavers toward our table,
wrapped in purple, if it only
gave a greeting, paused for grace,
I'd pour moonlight in its tumbler,
ladle stars onto its plate.

If this sleep, these bees behind my eyes,
would either grab or let me loose
I'd feed them pollen from my hand and
they would never have to go abroad again.
We'd live in peace, a swarm of dreamy songs,
or separated, they in their tree, I in mine.

If the malady wracking your body
breaks to sweat and swamps your eyes,
know that I'm beside you watching
for a daybreak dry as bee-sting
true to you as hunger stays
loyal to the crammed-up rows
of cans and bottles in our pantry.

Hush, pretty one, hush, be sure that if
bottled, bees rattle
like stomachs in hunger
or stars cast on a plate.

Sure

The sun that succumbed to the mudflats
some time around four in midwinter
was blue as an owl and now its power
to rouse us is gone, gone, like the nuclear
end-of-the-world. I'm glad you were sure.

The sure blue owl circled an earth
mouse-less as your mother's kitchen.
Moon-colored claws cupped the night air
angry and hungry. I'm glad.

Pure truth rose from the mudflats
rusted and covered with barnacles.
There you were with binoculars, shifting your view
from it to owl, from owl to it. I'm glad of your
witness,
glad you were sure.

Late Snow

In the space of all possible designs,
a particular day, a particular season,
June, and Thursday, in fact,
after morning bloomed gray and noon passed
in stupid silence, toward three
the snow fell, a glance of white
that blossomed once on phlox and yellow roses,
melted then, and disappeared.

Friday sunlight brought us back out to our gardens,
gloved in cotton, nerved with spades and shears,
while out there in the wilderness a desert pelican
rummaged in the dust of ancient ruins.

Snow and Starlight

As if snow would cover it.
As if the clouds up there
were tender, protective, a mother polar bear
lumbering to earth to warm her cubs

and I not avid for their fur.
As if there were protection from the snow.

As if stars were friendly,
lighting me to landfall, to a christchild,
grateful for the mercy, lost in night,
while angels round crouch to their errand,
sewing burial robes of whitest cloth.

Then so fierce is my want that I shall wear them,
observing fashion that I never liked nor understood,
as if the fallen snow were meant to warm me,
as if the stars knew where the starlight led.

Over and Under

Under water
sound turns color
and fish hear children squealing
yellow-green,
while green seaweed
navigate beneath a spectral ceiling
playing chromatic scales
on sea flute and viola d'amor.

Above sky
color turns water
and insects delight in new coolness,
melted blue,
while pilots who flew
to fiery deaths in our crusades
swim in the nude
like rambunctious children together.

No Fishing

What do you think
standing there, staring out to sea
in your enormous orange slicker?
That you're the chinook?

Maybe, after he's made it up river
when his teeth get long and his face gets black
and his back gets orange like that.

Fishing's over, feller,
time to go home and light the stove.
You're more like that coelacanth, anyway,
who everyone thought was long extinct
till he showed up, a twitching ghost,
at the bottom of an African boat.

Sunday in the Park with Josh

No dogs, no fish
cleaning, no
overnights,
no cooking, no fighting,
no litter, no spittle,
no smoke, no booze,
no deal, don't play
radios, roughhouse
or basketball.

It's bright blue Sunday
and I'm in the park
with my little Joshua
for our Sunday fun.

No fun —
goes, no yo-yos,
no overstress.
Stay trussed
in your carseat.
You must
wear a hardhat, and
it is suggested
as well, rubber gloves.

Pups

Open up! the pups have come
in yelping, rain-soaked disarray.
They've come a long and loathsome way
to eat your meat and gnaw your bones.
Open up! the pups have come.

Open up! the pups are here,
grim of muzzle, sore of paw.
They snarl for something warm and raw.
Oh see how those sharp teeth are bared.
Open up! the pups are here

in their cups again.

Open up, it's over now,
law's been and gone, the driveway's clear.
In fact it feels too quiet here.
Mercy, but that was a row.
Open up, it's over now.

Lessons from Nature

Just look outside
and listen, too!
there's much to learn
from what the birds
and bugs and fishes do.

The owl, he
will work all night
to satisfy
his appetite,

thus it would seem
the owl has
a lot of self esteem.

The bee with mud
makes her abode
cell by cell.
Everything the bee does
she does well.

If we are so
intelligent
should we not be at
least as diligent?

What the fish mean
down so deep
is difficult to interpret.

I haven't learned that much
from fish as yet,

but each creature has
an axiom to grind.
Next time you're outdoors
keep that in mind.

Fluff

If it's fluff I wear,
that's because burlap irritates my skin,
and when I itch I scratch
and when I scratch I can't pick up a pen.

I have been witness
to men and women acting at their worst.
I behave badly
myself often enough and am behaved against.

In a blue day
where gulls and gull-shadows appropriate the sky
with voracious grace,
they sanctify the earth in guano, pure lead white.

Your Flower

If she is your flower
firm and ferocious
snarling at winds that tousle and bend her

                    you be her tender

easily kneeling
your tender hands tamping the ground

                    and surround her

with romantic fingers your pokers and probes
caressing the smooth brave stem

                    the swelling of bulb

and pluck her
as fancy demands.

The Street

Red-white stripe of canopies can flap
above the street
happy as a heartbeat
packing scalloped lyrics in your brain
tap-dances in your feet.

You think:
They must have built engines
underneath these sidewalks
while I was asleep,

new-fangled cold fusion perpetual motion
machines to keep all of this going,

the way her pocketbook swings from her shoulder,
her silk scarf blowing.

Before Breakfast

Early morning
I pick up the news
from front steps so darkened by damp
as to make me think night
has spent itself quietly weeping.

Notebook: Cat, mice

Snowball lost her softness first
and then the fur itself. Her sight
went next and then her temper. Then she died.

In my kitchen mice go wild.
Their willful scratching fills the air
with a hilarity that's long been absent here.

Lumps

Three fishermen with ballooning nets
dip smelts. Eight huddled nuns
black habits flapping, watch.
The world suggests itself to us in lumps.

The world suggests itself to us in
clumps of flowered trees in summer,
clots of seabirds, bowls of oatmeal.
This is how its definition holds.

This is how its definition
binds the catechetical mind, knots its inquiries.
What will happen in vaporization?
How shall I know you? What will I find?

Good Throw

Stunned by stone, Goliath lies down
and grounds the kingdom of David.
We plant colored flags there
and wear more colors on our sleeves.
Listen to us whistling through our teeth,
whooo-ee, and clap and dance
to celebrate the good throw.
More than honor, more than beautiful faces,
we praise the accurate aim.

Oh, Bob Feller, Joe Montana, Sandy Koufax, oh.
Oh, intercontinental ballistic missile, oh.

Beach Combing

Heavens to Betsy,
the sun has turned pillow
the air become quilt.
Tillamook Bay laps like Jack at his bowl.
Not a scratch of wind, even the rocks
cushion my instep. This August day strolls
like Jack at my heel. We'll wade to our ankles,
search for agates and shells.

Eight o'clock now silvers the water.
We turn toward home, dragging our treasure:
rotten timber from a careless boat
and some rusty plumbing fixtures.

The Room You Want

I live in the room you want to rent,
stand at the window where you would stand
watching tubes of neon go from blue
to red, then yellow.

Pigeons loiter near the sill,
lift off as if with just one will
from a stained architrave here
to a similar ledge next door.

You don't see this occur. I do.
Birds in colored lights --
I hear them, too,
the thump accompanying the flight.

I turn back to the room
while evening seeps in,
noise now an irregular hum --
the voices of pedestrians,

one maybe yours, its tenor gruff
with rancor, also simple sadness.
If you continue long enough,
someone will listen, take your case,

like a debutante in a fast red car
zooming toward her charity bazaar.
She keeps a room deep in her heart
for life's wounded and soul-hurt.

She's not cardboard, after all,
and other people's miseries
are so conspicuous, they crawl
all around the streets of her city.

Besides, it's probable that I'll
grow restless soon. I usually do,
and check out in a thoughtless while
leaving behind a vacant room.

Then everybody gets a break,
you, the prudent deb, myself, and we'll
pursue our separate mistakes.
How proud we are of how we feel.

Opaque

Lake bottoms, those windows
of the cabin in the mountains
in winter with nobody there.
Nobody wants to exclaim at the view
"Like the top of the world!" nor anyone even
need look out.

Lady, hugged in a short fur coat,
walked her dog along Broadway, New York,
her throat already turned to grit.
Lake bottoms, her eyes.
Nobody could read them, although many claimed
to have tried.

Red

Red is the difficult color, voracious.
It wants to eat everything it touches.
We must learn to handle it.

An elderly man bought the little square hut
so long vacant.
I watched as he painted the front gate red,
short strokes with an inch-wide brush,
a slight tint of rust. He got it just right.

Sometimes in passing we speak of the weather.
I count him a friend.

Gray Day

On an ordinary, Oregon, overcast day,
one detail, two, may happen to shine
through the dark wet sand siding Alsea Bay.
I claim what I find as mine,

a bent spoon left in a flattened fort,
the give-away bubble from a hidden clam,
neon winks from a Japanese port,
a fallen star, Oz, I am

free to choose whatever I please
from these lucky luminosities.

Another Gray Day

Four clammers
bent into the mist that rises from the flats,
white stalks prodding the mud, buckets
squatting at their feet.

The afternoon is late, cold and damp.
One wears an emerald green jacket,
yellow muffler, yellow cap.
The clothes of the other three blend
into the brown and gray of the day.

Gulls swarm around them mewing for scraps,
although a few follow me along my way.
I always wonder how decisions are made.

DIAMONDS, DIAMONDS, DIAMONDS

Short Poems

"Your cousin mentioned that you wrote poems.
What kind of poems would that be?"
                                        asked he.

What kind?

"You know, what sort?"
                                Oh . . . short
I said, very short.   I write short poetry.
If I stand up straight I reach just five feet,
I try very hard, therefore, to keep
the heap of words within my reach.

            "Well, that's a relief," he said.

Bead Lady

As far as I know she strings beads all day,
day-glo colors on dental floss.
When she empties a cardboard box of beads
a hummingbird bird-like bird, she says,
deposits eggs there, and flies away.
A hummingbird bird-like bird, I said,
is a song, not a fact. There's no such thing.
Hmm, she replied, but it's green, blue and gold,
and it leaves me beads to string.

Busy

You'll have to wait. I have to eat,
then trim my nails and clean my teeth,
and bathe, then find a place to stow
leftover food and dirty clothes.

Wait. I want to catch my breath.
Impossible. I haven't yet
filled up enough of this grim day
to keep the wolf of memory at bay.

Aunts

The aunt I was telling you about?
                She died.
            They always do, these aunts,
and we must learn to carry on without them,
any of them, the favorites and the not so nice.
            It's the way of human life.
Myself, I plan for long and surprising times
ahead of me without the aunts,
                without their quirks and fancies,
                without their Christmas presents.
                    It simply makes good sense
to take the world, such as it is, as it is.
Remember I told you this aunt said she never lied?
                Wouldn't know how?
I wonder now if I should have taught her, or
                        at least made the offer.

Well, it's too late now.

Appreciation

        I like to rest
on one of the green benches
provided by the city
for its park.

        I like it best
in shade when the weather's hot
or a sunny spot in winter
if it happens that the sun comes out that day.

        A good city, this,
to lend someone like me
such a perch.

        I like the slats
that have a bit of spring to them.

        I like the fact
that often there's a paper left
so I can catch the news,

        I like the view
of others on their own slats,
sitting, making plans
for what to do next.

The Boys

In April I was ravenous,
my stomach thundered, my
mouth I daresay drooled.
I spread my skirt and purple figs
dropped into my lap,
and boys in baseball caps came by
back to work again
money to spend
on hot dogs, onion rings and fries.
I ate it all with room for more,
for figs, the boys, the world.

As I gray and
as I dry I
regret the gluttony,
but how make amends
to a fig's barren limbs
or regurgitate my dear boys.

Laid Up

I had the flu
and ran a fever.
That's when God appeared.

He was nice,
said it's all right
that I don't believe,

sat down on
a chair close by,
told priest and rabbi jokes

that he knew
I'd heard before.
Still, we giggled a lot.

I was giddily happy,
as if a child again,
sweating there in bed

like a warm float
in a backyard plastic
pool.

I'm well now,
my forehead cool,
and can't help wondering
what it is that draws him so
to miserable sick things.

Confusion of Childhood

When I was a little girl
during my quieter moments,
that is, when not making someone's day
miserable,
I mulled over philosophical ideas,
namely, God,
with much guesswork and perplexity.
Perhaps He's just a sort of spirit,
I reckoned,
an essence of benevolence,
justice made manifest.
Or maybe more like music,
the tune of the universe
permeating all of us.
Or like a thread?
that sews us all together, the good, the bad,
the alive and dead . . .

Such imaginings do addle
a child's curly head.
Thank God I finally know for sure.
He's an old man with a beard.

Sources

Betty, let's get to the bottom of things,
the invention of all our beliefs.
When you told me, "This time I am dying for sure,"
I back-pedaled with the best I could answer,
past catastrophes, and how
our escapes were probably undeserved.
(Underserved?" you asked.   Yes, that's what I meant,
not enough lemon tea, not enough cake.)
The original cake was intended for paste,
sugared for strength, to glue bridles on horses.
When everyone rode horses, remember,
we felt no need for traffic control.
Equine road-rage presented no problem.
Still, some folks were killed by mistake.
And some with purpose.   The first war
was especially deadly.   The first flag,
a foe's tattered hide,
hooked by accident,
flapping from a ten-foot spear.
People have died for a long time.   It's only new
when it's you, Betty.   I say that with ease.
The earliest cities were built by misfits,
overflow from the shady estates.
The game of baseball derives from an ad-hoc posse
who waited, fidgeted, then raced in circles rounding up
reactionaries.   The first neon sign
was an impolite outline, a finger thrust at the moon.
     The first
words spoken by friends: "What comes to me will
     come to you."

The Woods

Too many big trees,
mushrooms and brambles,
huckleberries, also: bears come here.
Butchers, those bears,
they tear up your heart. "There!"
they say "learn
to live with it ripped."

Daunted, I do so with patches, return,
stripped of tinsel and pride,
to the girdle of trees, Lord knows why.

You can't see the sky

nor more than four yards
in any direction. A bear
may be anywhere lurking, a smirk
on his jowls discerning my mulish
obtuse credulity.

The beast weighs heavy in his dark,
even as he sharpens claws on rough pine bark,
knows nothing of the daily rather I make
between the long white sidewalk heading outward
and his in-grown grove
that promises another, if disastrous,
still genuine, encounter.

Don't Leave Home Today

When the wind and rain subside

(someone might
    come across a bunch of light
    hiding under driftwood on the afterstorm beach,

    surreptitious
    bits of brittle phosphorus
    insinuating wisdom they don't intend to teach)

stay inside, stay inside.

Playing Cards

They're only playing-cards, yet
you clutch them to your scrawny breasts
and howl. What's with you anyway?
Either lay them down or else I'm breaking out
right now, no matter how loud you complain.
Look, you've made us threadbare,
played us naked -- I should stay around for more?
You can wallow in your swamp of tears till morning
if you want to with your diamonds, diamonds,
diamonds.

Only Look

Just look at her
bent over double
clutching her middle
to push in the hurt,
spent, derelict,
having loved herself sick
more love then more
having loved herself sore
measures the floor
from bedside to toilet
ignoring the doorbell
about, I'm afraid,
to love herself dead.

Afterthought

In latethought, maybe
it's so:
we were first made of clay.

No one goes
through seventy years
without seeing this way,

when mud squeezes
up
between the dear toes.

Boardwalk

The stalls were stocked with chocolate,
licorice and caramels.
The pelicans dripped with fish.
You wore a hat with bells.

The crowd smells of suntan oil,
the dock of mackerel.
There's that pelican again.
I wear a hat with bells.

What a pretty fare-thee-well,
two old slatterns dressed in bells.

Happily Ending

They said goodnight. They said goodbye.
They walked the porcupine and watched the moon.

The moon was bright, or would have been
had not the night clouds found a dogfight.

While dampened moonlight crashed through the
treetops
they walked the porcupine and talked in politic.

They talked erotic. One taught biology.
The other learned it. The talk was taut

and staticky, gunfire
coming in guts and starts.

No more the harmony that once engulfed them
like magnolia-scented salts in a warm bath.

Around the store fronts now ghosted empty,
they walked the porcupine, one so straight-
shouldered,

the other hunched. They turned a corner
into an avenue, their paces scraping

on the pavement as they reached the weathered stairs
to the porch. They stood apart

[95]

white-faced and hushed. They said goodnight.
They said goodbye. They stood quiet, in soapy quiet,

when somehow quite by accident one dropped the
leash.
In crackered moonlight, in sudden freedom

old Mr. Stickers trudged six steps down to his escape.
The other waved a lacy handkerchief

and waved again to wave him on through hasty night
but never turned aside, that when a bird rasped

from foreign branches its best glory,
they said good morning.

A Declaration of Faith

Where prayers are effective,
springs gush forth and sequined fishes
swim over sand. Where crying works,
fishes swim over the sand to paupers, handing out
hooks,
where crying works and prayers are heard.

Where Americans care
and drive to their fellowships,
trees shoot up out of slash to protect them
shading them gently. Gently shaded
from cancerous sunlight, new possums are born
from tire treads, where Americans care.

When we meet together
to sing, holding hands in a circle,
fish-full streetpeople leap from the shadows to join us
and sweet baby possums play at our feet.

Pantheist

From an overhanging limb
Nature spoke to him.
"Sweet, sweet, sweet," it said
And he believed each word.

On the way to where he worked
He passed St. Andrew's church.
It called out "Ding, dang, dell,"
Which he believed as well.

When he reached the factory
With its looming chimney,
Came a whisper "Puh, puh, puh."
"Amen," he answered, looking up.

In nonce, fixed, and open forms, Jean Esteve's poems give us a wry, witty, darkly ironic music. Her restive, often grimly festive voice gives us talk that's "…taut / and staticky, gunfire / coming in guts and starts." Esteve offers hymns to oddness, songs of the world seen askance. In this first full-length collection, she *becomes* a winter sun, claiming as her own whatever catches and reflects some of her light — her poems a celebration of those "lucky luminosities."

---Paulann Petersen, Oregon Poet Laureate

These poems are perfect cocktails of knowledge, oddity, brevity, humor, and rhyme. They are surprisingly subtle and stand up to being read again and again. They also successfully belie the received notion that heavily-rhymed poems are only useful for nursery rhymes and light verse. With each rereading, these deftly rhymed poems seem smarter and smarter, and more wryly subversive.

— Mary Jo Bang, Judge, Oregon Book Awards, comments on Jean Esteve's chapbook *Off-Key*

Jean Esteve is one of my favorite poets, right along in with Dickinson, Frost, Roethke, May Sarton and more. Not that she is like any of those-- Esteve is not like any other poet namable. Her poems are a distillation of dry observation, of odd quirky language, and of a vision that comes from an odd angle of light. I never tire of reading her work-- I

come to a familiar poem, and find it fresh all over
again.

--Ruth F. Harrison, author of *How Singular and Fine*

In her fine new collection, Jean Esteve makes the
familiar strange – and the strange, familiar. Her
poems pivot and dart like the mind's restless eye.
They startle and stun.

Mostly short, but never small, these poems pulse with
sound play, puns and rhyme. Don't expect lullabys or
lip balm. Hold on: Be ready to feel a little off-balance,
precarious. Esteve's poems are quirky little
comeuppances. They contain both trouble and fun,
blind alleys and "lucky luminosities" – stars of all
kinds. Joe Montana and Sandy Koufax appear. So do
Goliath and God, a jocular presence who tells priest
and rabbi jokes. The surrealist painter Magritte
shows up, with his pipe that may not be a pipe.

I hear echoes of Gertrude Stein and e e cummings, but
the voice is distinctly Esteve's. Many of her poems
are set along the north Oregon coast near Tillamook,
with its mudflats and floodtides, its pelicans and
crows, the sky full of rough weather. Still, there's that
winter sun, "silky and thin…like lady's lingerie." And
then, as April nears, "this measured allowance of
daffodils breaking through cracks in the pavement."

—Don Colburn, author of *Because You Might Not
Remember*